Martha's Vineyard

Martha's Vineyard

HOUSES AND GARDENS

Photographs by Lisl Dennis
Text by Polly Burroughs

With additional photographs by
Alison Shaw, Mark Lovewell, Katherine Rose, and Bruce T. Martin

Little, Brown and Company
BOSTON TORONTO LONDON

First Edition

Additional photographs by: Alison Shaw, pages 152,
155 (bottom right), 166, 170; Mark Lovewell, pages 11
(right), 16, 98, 100; Katherine Rose, page 196 (right);
Bruce T. Martin, page 84.

Library of Congress Cataloging-in-Publication Data

Dennis, Lisl.
    Martha's Vineyard: houses and gardens / photographs by
Lisl Dennis; text by Polly Burroughs. — 1st ed.
    p.   cm.
    ISBN 0-316-18083-1
    1. Martha's Vineyard (Mass.) — Description and travel —
Views.   2. Dwellings — Massachusetts — Martha's
Vineyard — Pictorial works.   3. Interior decoration —
Massachusetts — Martha's Vineyard — Pictorial works.
4. Gardens — Massachusetts — Martha's Vineyard —
Pictorial works.   I. Burroughs, Polly.
II.   Title.
F72.M5D37   1992   91-38322

10   9   8   7   6   5   4   3   2   1

IMAGO

Design by Janis Owens

Published simultaneously in Canada by Little, Brown
& Company (Canada) Limited

Printed in Hong Kong

With gratitude to my aunt and uncle, Dave and Ann Taylor, for their support of my career.

L.D.

For Rick, Nancy, my grandchildren, Nicholas Loring and Hannah Grinnell, and that dog, Scup.

P.B.

Contents

———— ◆ ————

I wish to thank Laurie White, my dedicated and tireless photography assistant, and Mariko Kawaguchi from Donaroma Nursery for her inspired flower arrangements. I am most grateful to Jennifer Josephy, my editor at Little, Brown and Company, for her support in this project and to Polly Burroughs for finding so many wonderful houses for me to photograph. Finally, I especially want to thank all the homeowners for allowing me to come into their busy summer lives.

L.D.

My thanks to Arthur Thornhill, Jr., for introducing us to Little, Brown; to Mariko Kawaguchi for her exquisite flower arrangements; to Paula DelBonis for her expert typing; to Eulalie Regan, *Vineyard Gazette* librarian; to Richard Reston, editor and publisher of the *Vineyard Gazette*, for his help above and beyond the call of friendship; to Alison Shaw, Katherine Rose, and Mark Lovewell, who were so thoughtful and helpful; and to Jennifer Josephy, senior editor at Little, Brown, whose patience, insight, and expertise were extraordinary.

To gather the necessary information for a house and garden book covering three centuries also requires the kindness and help of friends and acquaintances. Arthur Railton, Eulalie Regan, Lane Lovell, and Kenneth Deitz were extremely helpful in advising me on historical matters. I would also like to express my appreciation to John Gadowski, Jeff Verner, Karen Ward, Betty Hitesman, Ann Crumm, Ann Taylor, Ann Fulton, Nancy Burroughs, Helen Bowring, and Earle Radford. I am particularly indebted to Carolyn Verbeck, whose wonderful suggestions and assistance — all along the way — were invaluable.

P.B.

Introduction

One of the most compelling features of any island resort is that not only does it provide an escape, both physical and psychological, from urban America, it also imparts a strong sense of place in unique small towns and villages. On Martha's Vineyard, the extraordinary beauty of the geological terrain further contributes to the Island's enormous popularity. The broad windswept beaches, the snug harbors teeming with boats, the charming historic towns with their neat white houses and period gardens, the fields covered with wildflowers, the thick woodlands, the green ribbons of marsh grasses fringing Island ponds, the handsome contemporary houses tucked under hillsides alongshore or capping hilltops, the timeless lure of the sea itself — all of these make this one of the most popular summer resorts anywhere.

It is the blending of the historic with the contemporary that gives each of the Island's distinct communities its own individuality and character: the formality of the stately whaling captains' houses facing Edgartown Harbor; the holiday frivolity of Oak Bluffs' boardwalk atmosphere and charming gingerbread architecture; the dignity of East Chop's handsome Shingle Style houses on the bluff overlooking Vineyard Sound; the bustling commerce of Vineyard Haven, with its handsome nineteenth-century houses fanning out toward the large turn-of-the-century summer cottages along the West Chop bluff; the informality of North and West Tisbury, where working farms exist side by side with Colonial reproductions and modern summer houses; the tranquillity of Chilmark, where large contemporary houses perch on the high, rolling hills where huge flocks of sheep once roamed the moors, and old, weathered farmhouses dot the landscape; the beauty and sense of heritage of Gay Head, home of the Wampanoag Indians, whose history is so closely linked to that of the Island; and the harmony of the tiny port of Menemsha, where the old and the new — the fishing fleet and modern yachts, the ancestral homes of the fishermen and new cottages — blend together seamlessly.

The Island is twenty miles long and ten miles wide at its broadest point, with a terrain as varied as the individual character of its six towns. A high, boulder-strewn ridge runs all along the North Shore, extending to the moors and cliffs at Gay Head, the Island's western tip. The flat outwash plains of mid-Island, formed by melting glacial ice, stretch to the windswept Atlantic Ocean, where fingerlike ponds reach inward from

the sea. Strips of marshland surround both these estuaries and others on the northern side of the Island, providing a haven for marine and bird life. Four picturesque harbors are carved into the Nantucket and Vineyard Sound side.

It was not this beautiful and varied landscape but rather the vegetation that fascinated the British explorer Captain Bartholomew Gosnold, who in 1602 became the first European to discover the Island. While he noted in his report that the strawberries "were bigger than ours in England" and also mentioned the familiar blueberry and raspberry bushes, it was the masses of grapevines that most impressed him: "such an incredible store of vines, as well in the woodie part of the Island where they run upon every tree, as on the outward parts, that we could not goe for treading upon them." Historians believe Gosnold named the island Martha's Vineyard in honor of his daughter and possibly of his mother-in-law, Martha Golding.

It was nearly half a century later, in 1641, that Thomas Mayhew of Watertown, Massachusetts, purchased the Vineyard, Nantucket, and the Elizabeth Islands for forty pounds from two English noblemen who had conflicting grants for the islands. The following year Mayhew's son arrived on the Vineyard with a group of settlers and chose Edgartown for the first white settlement.

The tiny community grew slowly at first. The settlers' first houses are typified by an example that still stands in Edgartown, the one-story Cape with its deep shed roof located behind Edgartown's Old Whaling Church. The design of this seventeenth-century house is based on a style from Devon and Cornwall in England.

Gradually other settlements sprang up around the Island. The early settlers were farmers and fishermen, but as time went on, the Islanders turned more and more to the sea for their livelihood. The growth of Tisbury, or Vineyard Haven, began with the expansion of maritime trade between the colonies and the West Indies. Cranberries, wool, salt cod, and clay from the Vineyard's North Shore were exported to the mainland through Vineyard Haven, and the port itself, only five miles from the shoulder of Cape Cod, became a primary anchorage for ships moving up and down the Eastern Seaboard, maintaining that status until the Cape Cod Canal was built, in 1914.

The port's prosperity in the nineteenth century was largely responsible for Vineyard Haven's handsome Colonial and Greek Revival buildings, just as in Edgartown, profits from the whaling industry enabled sea captains and others to build large, elegant houses in various architectural styles.

Oak Bluffs was originally a Methodist Camp Meeting place where the devout would congregate each summer to pitch their tents in a grove of oak trees and attend services, but by the 1870s it was also the Island's first summer resort town. The invention of the jigsaw and the fretsaw made possible the Carpenter Gothic architecture that festoons the town like a rainbow-colored, lacy Valentine, adorning cottages with turrets, rococo scrollwork, tiny balconies, and Gothic windows.

Summer houses were also being built at East Chop and West Chop during this period, and Edgartown's first resort hotel soon opened at Katama, on the South Shore. The towns at the western end of the Island — North Tisbury and West Tisbury, Chilmark, Menemsha, and Gay Head — were fishing and farming communities and did not become popular with summer visitors until much later. Artists, writers, and academics who rented inexpensive shacks and cottages were the first to summer in these areas.

The evolving architecture of the Island mirrored design changes taking place on the mainland. Builders who used design books frequently combined disparate styles, and often one period overlapped another. During the China Trade period, many houses were filled with lovely examples of decorative art; exquisite porcelains, furniture, textiles, and artwork were brought home on whaling ships and other vessels from ports in the Pacific as well as in Europe. Fruit trees and vegetable seeds were also imported, as were numerous decorative plants and herbs, including boxwood and ivy from England; Scotch broom, with its buttercup-yellow flowers, which have since spread all over the Island; the rugosa rose of Japanese origin, whose bright blossoms now blanket long stretches of sandy beach; hybrid roses, many of which thrive in the Island's climate, beautifying formal gardens and tumbling over fences and stone walls; Edgartown's famous pagoda tree, which arrived in a flowerpot; and Japanese umbrella pines. Today many homeowners combine the native and the exotic in their gardens and landscaping — in both formal planting and, more often, informal cottage gardens and wildflower fields.

The growing popularity of the Island as a summer resort over the years has prompted an increasing concern for preserving wildlife areas in their natural state. The pioneer in this visionary effort was the late Henry Beetle Hough, owner and editor of the *Vineyard Gazette* for nearly half a century. Many organizations are now involved in preservation, and over 16 percent of the Island's landmass has been set aside forever: marshes, open rolling fields that reach down to touch the sea, beaches, and freshwater ponds will be left in perpetuity to nature — to the rhythms of the seasons and the sea.

These wildlife sanctuaries not only protect birds, animals, and plant life, they also enable the visitor to envision the Island in its natural state. Because of the Vineyard's proximity to the Gulf Stream, all sorts of unusual plants thrive in its temperate climate. Wave upon wave of native wildflowers blanket the fields in summer, and pine trees, sculpted close to the ground by the relentless winds, dot the landscape. The hardy beach plum takes root everywhere, masses of grapevines cover stone walls, huge pink mallow bursts into bloom in the wetlands, a palette of asters, goldenrod, and Queen Anne's lace colors the meadows in August, and the sweet fragrance of wild rose, swamp azalea, and sweet pepper bush is so strong that it startled the early explorers, who made note of it in their ships' logs and reports.

It is the balance between the old and the new — between the wildlife sanctuaries and the villages with their manicured gardens, between the old houses that have witnessed so much of the Island's history and the handsome contemporary homes surrounded by fields of wildflowers or hidden in the woods — that gives the Vineyard its diversified character. Underlying the inevitable changes is the eternal fascination of the many moods and mystical nature of the ocean itself — the anchor to windward — for it is the wind and the sea that have shaped and reshaped the Island's shores, molded its history, and provided its inhabitants with their livelihood for centuries.

VINEYARD SOUND

ATLANTIC
OCEAN

Cape Ann

Boston

Plymouth

CAPE COD
BAY

BUZZARDS BAY

Nantucket

*Martha's
Vineyard*

Lambert's
Cove

WEST TISBURY

North Tisbury .

West Tisbury .

CHILMARK

. Menemsha

Lobsterville .

. Gay Head

GAY HEAD

*Menemsha
Pond*

Chilmark .

*Squibnocket
Pond*

G. W. Ward

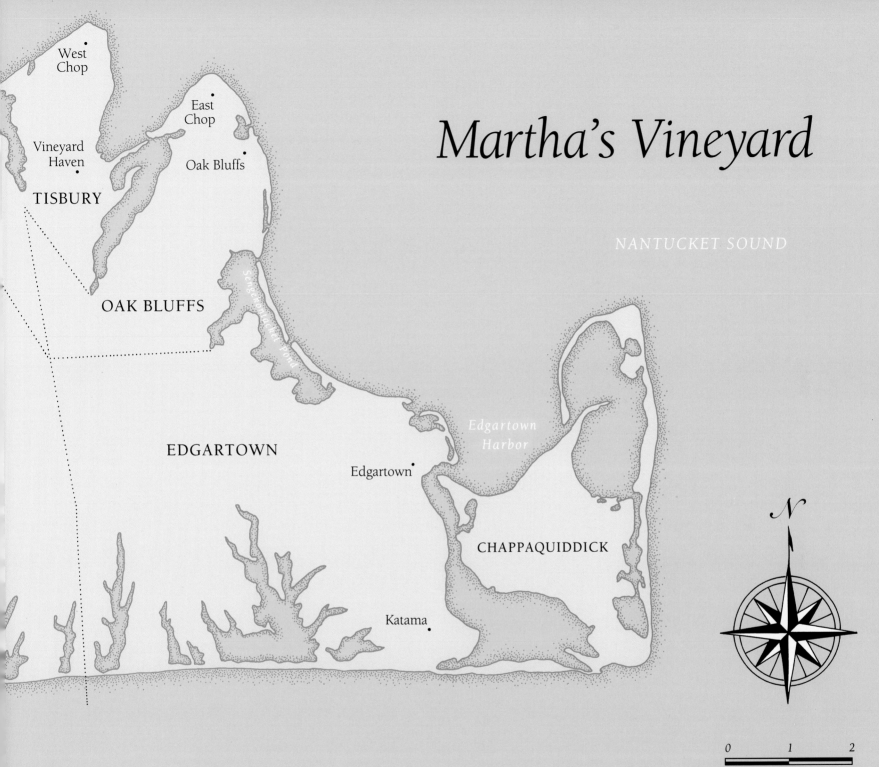

Martha's Vineyard

West
Chop

Vineyard
Haven

TISBURY

East
Chop

Oak Bluffs

OAK BLUFFS

Sengekontacket Pond

NANTUCKET SOUND

EDGARTOWN

Edgartown

*Edgartown
Harbor*

CHAPPAQUIDDICK

Katama

ATLANTIC OCEAN

N

```
0        1        2
━━━━━━━━━━━━━━━━━━━━
         MILES
```

Down-Island

—

VINEYARD HAVEN

WEST CHOP

EAST CHOP

OAK BLUFFS

EDGARTOWN

CHAPPAQUIDDICK

Captain Gilbert Smith House

——◆——

VINEYARD HAVEN

In the mid–nineteenth century, many handsome Greek Revival houses were built in what is now Vineyard Haven's historic district, up the hill behind Main Street. Vineyard Haven was a thriving coastal port at the time, with three out of every four of its male inhabitants working as either merchant seamen or whalemen. After spending twenty-five years whaling in the Arctic Ocean, Captain Gilbert Smith bought this large house, built around 1850, on his retirement.

It was not whaling but rather three enormously successful illustrated cookbooks that enabled Susan Branch, a charming young native Californian, to purchase the house in 1989. While it did not require any restoration, Susan and Joe Hall, manager of the Black Dog restaurant in Vineyard Haven, furnished and redecorated the place. He is interested in collecting old prints, books, and furniture, while she chose the lace, linens, china, and glass, both of them endowing the rooms with their cheerful personalities. "We complement each other, both in furnishing the house and in our mutual interest in cooking," Susan explains.

The handsome front door, with lace-curtained sidelights and antique carriage lights on the pilasters, is decorated with a basket of cosmos and zinnias. The curving handrails combine with the vernacular Doric columns and the pots of pink geraniums to make a charming, inviting doorway.

3

The living room is a mixture of the old and the new. On and above the handsome mantel are prints from Joe Hall's collection, with, at the far end, a pair of antique brass candlesticks; in the foreground is an English Queen Anne stool.

The red and white china in the corner cupboard
on the left and on the dining-room table is
Copeland Spode's Tower English, from Susan's
china collection. Susan arranged the peonies and
tiger lilies and prepared the dessert tea, which
includes chocolate truffles, cookies, strawberry
angel-food cake, and fresh fruit served with Earl
Grey tea. The lace curtains were made from an
old tablecloth. Susan and Joe, always on the
lookout for acquisitions for the house, bought the
dining-room chairs at an auction.

Preparations for a delicious summer lunch of fresh corn, steamed lobsters, mussels, and clams, stuffed tomatoes, tossed salad, French bread, and white wine.

Lunch is served in a delightful rose-covered pergola in the backyard.

7

The enormous backyard is edged by conifers and old-fashioned flowering shrubs and trees that create a fairyland of scents and blossoms in the spring, including lilacs, weeping cherry, dogwood, magnolia, wisteria, old roses, hydrangeas, mock orange, English holly, blue spruce, white birch, and others.

Left: Joe Hall built the fenced-in vegetable and flower garden with raised beds. The white picket fence is encircled by sweet peas, Susan's favorite flower.

The master bedroom has touches of Susan's lace collection in the curtains and the lace canopy on the antique four-poster bed. Her Minton china is used here for a hearty breakfast.

The Old Seamen's Bethel

VINEYARD HAVEN

The long arm of shoreline that runs from Vineyard Haven out to the West Chop lighthouse fronts many summer and year-round houses. In the early nineteenth century, several small settlements were clustered along the shore; one of these included sea captains' houses with their traditional workshops, a commercial wharf, a ship's chandlery, and the original Seamen's Bethel, an organization that tended to the needs of sailors in port and that was later moved to the center of Vineyard Haven.

Mike Wallace of "60 Minutes" has summered on the Island since he was a child. When he bought the Seamen's Bethel in 1988 from Mrs. Kingman Brewster, widow of the former president of Yale University and United States ambassador to England, many changes had already been made to the old building. Mike and Mary Wallace have undertaken further renovations, including the conversion of a small warren of rooms in the rear of the house into a large family room/kitchen.

A view of the lawn at the back of the house, which stretches down to the waterfront, shows the archway and steps leading to the circular driveway. The large guest wing on the right is for children and grandchildren; on the left is the new family room/kitchen, with master bedroom above. An arrangement of peach godetia and yellow tansy adds a spot of color.

The chairs on the lawn (seen here from the driveway, through the archway separating the guest wing from the main house) and the kitchen window nearby afford, according to Mary Wallace, "our favorite views. We love to watch the ferries come and go."

Seen from the dining room, an interplay of periods and fabrics is evident in the Wallaces' living room, which opens onto a screened porch with views of Vineyard Haven's outer harbor, East Chop, and Cape Cod. Mary Wallace did her own decorating; the Victorian sofa and chair are family pieces that she brought up from New York, while the coffee table by the fireplace is an English reproduction. The blues of sea and sky in the print over the reproduction mantel, of the United States steamship President, blend with the light-blue walls. The coffee table in front of the contemporary sofa was made by a Vineyard craftsman; on it is a bouquet of lavender and blue hydrangeas, ivy foliage, and silver artemisia.

Mary Wallace enjoys painting furniture and other decorative arts. She marbleized the top and sponge-painted the legs of this simple Italian table, which holds a spectacular arrangement of lavender larkspur, blue and lavender hybrid delphinium, lavender asters, blue agapanthus, pink lilies, and bear grass.

With three generations in and out of the house all summer, the Wallaces' dock is a busy place; some family members go clamming, while others prefer to take out the sailing dinghy, which is usually tied up alongside.

Shades of blue, a favorite country color, predominate on the large screened-in porch, which stretches across the waterfront side of the house. On the end table at left is a blue butterfly-weed plant; on the right is a planting of white feverfew, blue ageratum, silver dusty miller, white yarrow, and pteris fern. In the background, Chinese Chippendale–style chairs surround a table where the Wallaces often have lunch or dinner overlooking the harbor.

The Loy House

WEST CHOP

Cradling Vineyard Haven Harbor on either side are two headlands, called East Chop and West Chop. West Chop began to be developed as a summer colony in the late nineteenth century, when a group of Bostonians built large Shingle Style houses along the bluff. The development continued into the twentieth century, when Frank and Dale Loy's big, comfortable house was constructed. The Loys, residents of Washington, D.C., where Frank Loy heads a foundation, bought the house in 1981 and have furnished it in a delightful informal style.

The rugged, stony point of land at the tip of West Chop is punctuated by large Shingle Style "cottages," built at the turn of the century.

The large dining room is furnished with casual
country antiques. Although Dale Loy is an artist
whose work has been included in many group
and individual shows at the National Academy
of Sciences, the Corcoran Gallery, and else-
where, she prefers to decorate her walls here
with old gameboards that complement the
furnishings. Sunflowers and multicolored cosmos
from the garden await arranging.

The front hall is furnished with an old flour
chest and pine settee that the owners found in
Washington.

Just off the kitchen is a display of the owners'
collection of antique toys and games.

Far left: *The comfortable living room, which suits the owners' summer life-style, features a Victorian rocker, an old pine weaver's bench, a knife box filled with hydrangeas, and Windsor chairs by the fire.*

Left: *A collage of objects from Dale Loy's collection of old fabrics contains a star-shaped pincushion, a Victorian coverlet, and a charming pillow made from pieces of old quilts found in antique shops.*

Below: *The front porch, furnished with a mixture of country antiques and traditional wicker, looks out across Vineyard Sound to East Chop.*

Colossal Fossil

———◆———

EAST CHOP

Sited on a high bluff overlooking the sea in East Chop, this expansive house was built in 1890 for Fran Ferris, head of the New York Chamber of Commerce, and reflected a new taste for summer living in one's own place rather than in a huge family hotel. One of many houses in Oak Bluffs and East Chop that were originally inspired by the design of medieval English country cottages with their complex rooflines and towers, it was intended to resemble an ancient castle and is known locally as Colossal Fossil. The tower is topped by an osprey weather vane made by local craftsman Travis Tuck.

Richard and Sage Chase of Connecticut bought the house in 1982 and with a few renovations restored it to its original grandeur to accommodate their large family. Mrs. Chase completely redecorated the interior in her own colorful, whimsical, and relaxed style.

White oxeye daisies and crown vetch, which prevent soil erosion on steep banks like these on the bluff, prove an irresistible lure on a summer day. Working from an old photograph, the owners had the second-floor porches restored to their original configuration.

Wild coreopsis and deep-blue salvia fill a meadow in the foreground. The wrap-around veranda completely encircles this stunning Victorian Queen Anne–style shingle house.

A grouping of vintage wicker furniture provides comfortable seating on the extraordinary wrap-around porch. The house's exterior color scheme of soft pink and sea-foam gray is carried through to the porch, where it serves to accent both the elaborate architectural detail overhead and the unusual curved siding. Trailing pink geraniums grow in the hanging planters, and trailing ivy sprouts in the planter on the coffee table. Large verandas such as this represented one of the first steps toward outdoor living before the advent of decks and terraces after World War II.

Left: An acrylic triptych of geraniums and columns, adapted from the porch decor and painted by a member of the family, hangs over the living-room settee. A rag rug anchors the room, pulling the antique wicker rockers into an intimate circle. The roses and cosmos on the coffee table are from Mrs. Chase's garden.

Mrs. Chase collects colorful, whimsical pottery, examples of which may be seen here, on the dining-room table and in the china cupboard. The ladderback chairs, as well as most of the other furnishings, came with the house. The dining room opens into the living room, with its bright, summery colors and its view of Nantucket Sound through the French doors.

Left: In the front hall, the original mantelpiece was too tall and had to be lowered. Blue European tiles were used for the fireplace surround and the hearth. Mrs. Chase found the fireboard, decorated with hydrangeas, in Nantucket; echoing the painted theme, pink geraniums and begonias fill white baskets in front.

The master bedroom, under the eaves, is Mrs. Chase's favorite room, especially when "in the late afternoon the colors of the sea seem to come inside." All of the bedrooms in the house have prints and white organdy curtains, and most have old iron beds that came with the house and have been repainted.

One of the boys' rooms, with a Victorian bureau and mirror and an old oil lamp that has been electrified. Attics were omitted in these houses, so all the top-floor rooms are situated directly under the eaves, leaving the architectural details and the traditional bead and board siding open to view. One of the Chases' sons' tennis trophies are displayed on the bureau; the son himself, meanwhile, has been at work repainting the window trim.

Right: All the walls, furniture, floors, and ceilings in the house have been painted bright white. The downstairs guest room is furnished with a charming Victorian bureau and a vintage wicker chair, and brightened with roses from the owners' garden, which was redone along with the house.

Oak Bluffs

Methodism made its first appearance on the Island in 1787, with the arrival of John Saunders, an ex-slave from Virginia who lived and preached in Eastville, part of East Chop. By 1835 it had become so popular that a permanent place of worship was established at the present Camp Ground in Oak Bluffs, with a speaker's stand encircled by tents to accommodate the rapidly increasing flock of believers. Most came for only a few weeks, but many were eager to stay longer, in more permanent dwellings. When the first prefabricated Carpenter Gothic cottage was brought over from Rhode Island in 1859 to replace a tent, it set off a building frenzy that coincided with the invention of the jigsaw and the band saw. Builders worked day and night to keep up with the demand, and owners vied with one another to have the most elaborate wedding-cake facades: gables, turrets, spires, scrollwork under the eaves, Gothic windows, tiny balconies, and fancy-cut shingles adorned their lilliputian cottages. These lacy Valentines were then painted in vivid rainbow hues. The community soon attracted a secular population as well, and by the 1870s huge wooden hotels and large, romantic Queen Anne–style and Carpenter Gothic houses had sprung up around the village. More than fifteen side-wheelers steamed into port each day to unload visitors eager to enjoy the elegant "watering place."

To mark the closing of the season of religious meetings each year, the Methodists held Illumination Night, during which each tent was required to keep a lantern lit. In the 1870s a Japanese merchant began selling elaborate paper lanterns to celebrate the occasion, and their popularity, as well as Illumination Night itself, continues today.

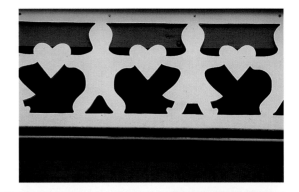

Kelly House

———◆———

OAK BLUFFS

During the Victorian era, an industrial revolution brought prosperity to the middle class and spawned a building boom in Oak Bluffs, which became a landmark site for neo-Rococo- or neo-Gothic-style architecture, also called Carpenter Gothic or simply gingerbread. The tiny houses on the Campground and other, much larger ones around the village all have lacy, wedding-cake exteriors, with fancy-cut shingles, cathedral windows, gables, and turrets.

John and Sharon Kelly, Connecticut residents, bought their house on their first weekend visit to the Island, in 1977. Built by the Oak Bluffs Land Company in the 1860s, during the town's building boom, it is a fine example of the eclectic blending of the high Victorian Queen Anne and American Carpenter Gothic styles, with protruding bays, wrap-around verandas, and an Italianate tower. The house was decrepit when the Kellys bought it; extensive exterior restoration was necessary, as was a complete redecoration of the interior, much of which the Kellys did themselves. They also began a tireless search for Victorian furnishings.

The guest room opens onto a small porch overlooking the gazebo in nearby Ocean Park (where weekly band concerts are held in summer) and the center of town.

The front of the house, with its hip-roofed gable and intricate trim.

Old beaded evening bags, with butterfly wings in a 1980 Oak Bluffs Centennial Cup Plate.

The living room radiates turn-of-the-century charm. On the original fireplace wall are two plaster Victorian sconces, an old wooden clock, the owners' collection of Japanese porcelain, and a pair of period landscapes. The wicker furniture dates from the early 1900s; a fern, so typical of that time, rests on a wind-up Victrola in one corner. On the near table is a tea set from the Kellys' large collection of Nippon china. A bouquet of silver dollar, tansy, eucalyptus, yellow gerbera, and zinnia brightens the coffee table.

An unusual canvas cornice frieze, hand-painted in France, encircles the dining room. The 1920s Empire-style table, which is large enough to seat sixteen, is decorated with a vase full of silver dollar, rubrum lilies, and eucalyptus leaves.

Right: A porcelain sink, made in England in the 1870s, is used as a bar in the dining room, adorned with a pair of antique white cinnabar vases.

Off the front hall is the billiard room, with its massive slate-top oak billiard table. The table, which was original to the house, was built by Brunswick in 1897 and had to be completely restored. Sharon Kelly made the stained-glass windows herself.

On the period mantelpiece in this guest room are an unusual hand-painted wooden clock, made in 1880 by the Sessions Clock Company, and a pair of Japanese porcelain plates. The owners found the print over the claw-foot bathtub (in background) in Paris.

Left: *The antique Nippon cabbage-rose vase atop the old oak bureau is filled with orange tea roses, lavender statice, hydrangea, and sedum 'Autumn Joy'.*

Right: *On the bureau is a wisteria-decorated Oriental vase filled with purple iris, lavender larkspur, magenta miniature gladiolus, wisteria, peach yarrow, and variegated euonymus. The miniature floribunda roses, pansies, and old-fashioned dianthus in the small vases echo other colors in the room.*

38

The Kellys' collection of antique clocks is on view throughout the house; this French porcelain clock, made by the Ansonia Clock Company, rests on a guest-room mantel.

Another guest room is decorated with a late-nineteenth-century landscape, a clock (one of the very few reproductions in the house), and a period oak rocker. The owners also collect old magazines and lace.

Edgartown

———◆———

Edgartown's most elegant houses, located in the center of the village, were built with whaling money in the early and mid-nineteenth century. Most of them are Greek Revival in style, though many may properly be classified as transitional, meaning that they combine the delicate detailing of the earlier Federal period — characterized by balustrades on the porticos and roofs — with Greek Revival's fluted Doric or plain square columns, sidelights, and open or filled-in fanlights. The majority of the houses were originally painted white in imitation of the white limestone used in Greek temples; the tradition is carried on today.

Thomas Cooke House

———◆———

EDGARTOWN

Squire Thomas Cooke, a successful Edgartown businessman and politician, built this handsome Colonial Georgian house in the 1780s. It is now owned by Vice Admiral and Mrs. Allen Mayhew Shinn, having been in Vice Admiral Shinn's family for four generations. His great-grandmother, a direct descendant of the Vineyard's founding family, the Mayhews, acquired the house in 1835.

The structure was built at a time when chimneys were being put at both ends rather than in the middle of a house, allowing for a gracious central hall. The frame surrounding the front door, with sidelights, was a later addition. The Shinns have undertaken minor renovations, including combining two rooms to make a rear living room and attaching two small original outbuildings to the main structure. The house is a historical treasure, filled with wonderful antiques that have come down through the family and other objects collected by the present owners on their world travels. The grounds have been completely redone and are beautifully planted with lush green everywhere.

Both of the Shinns are gardeners, and the small outbuilding annexed to the kitchen of the main house serves as their garden shop, filled with flowerpots, tools, and other supplies.

The living room is to the left of the front hall in this four-square house. Many of the furnishings either came with the house or are old family pieces, including the Victorian chair, the unsigned oil painting of a horse (which was in Mrs. Shinn's family), and the antique brass sconces. On top of the antique desk-bookcase is a Spanish ship model, and inside it are two Japanese Satsuma plates that the Shinns found on their travels. The colors of the Oriental rug are reflected in a Chinese vase, which is filled with orange tiger lilies, bloodleaf maple, white viburnum, coreopsis, and blue brodiaea. An antique Chinese chess set and a Ching dynasty vase decorate the mantel. None of the fireplaces in the house had a fire surround until about 1800, when the mantels were added to the plain paneled walls.

The oil portrait in the dining room, which is just to the right of the front hall, depicts Vice Admiral Shinn's great-grandmother Mayhew. The mid-eighteenth-century grandfather clock, made by Nathaniel Edwards of Acton, Massachusetts, is Mrs. Shinn's favorite piece in the house. The large arrangement on the table includes fruit and flowers: grapes, apples, pears, Bing cherries, sunflowers, burgundy astilbe, purple lisianthus, anemones, burgundy and coral renanthera orchid, 'James Storei' orchids, orange spiky montebretia, dianthus, and purple iris.

Right: Another family portrait is of James Mathewson of Providence, Rhode Island, who was Mrs. Shinn's great-grandfather. The charger is part of Mrs. Shinn's collection of Imari porcelain; it and the painted wooden Ching dynasty figures rest on an eighteenth-century chest that came with the house. The tiny arrangements contain yellow and mauve ranunculus, red floribunda roses, blue brodiaea, purple anemone, and dianthus.

Upstairs, at the back of the house, is Vice Admiral Shinn's office, filled with a collection of artifacts from the Shinns' worldwide travels. A Philippine bolo knife can be seen above the framed certificate; in front of it are, from left to right, a Hindu war shield, a tasseled Japanese short sword, an antique postage scale, and a Chinese abacus. On the shelf below, a Japanese abacus is placed next to a model of Vice Admiral Shinn's former command, the U.S.S. Forrestal. In the foreground is an old backgammon set.

The view into a guest room from the upstairs front hall, with a Windsor rocking chair on the left. Beneath the Victorian mirror are a pair of yellow Chinese vases and a bowl of orange tiger lilies, orange daylilies, silver artemisia, yellow ranunculus, and coreopsis.

In the master bedroom a cloissoné bowl full of peonies, lace cap and Nikko hydrangeas, and white viburnum decorates the Victorian bureau, along with a collection of old family daguerreotypes.

Tiger lilies and red floribunda roses tumble over the fence in the brick courtyard.

One of Mrs. Shinn's favorite settings is this garden room with its Cambodian statue of Vishnu, known as the "Preserver," surrounded by impatiens, astilbe, hosta, and laurel.

Miniscule

———◆———

EDGARTOWN

Built in 1750 by Matthew Mayhew, this Georgian Colonial is one of the most elegant houses on the Edgartown waterfront. The former owner, Miss Frances Louise Meikleham, and her mother, who founded the Martha's Vineyard Garden Club, put in a sunken geometric garden in the shape of a Union Jack. Miss Meikleham was the great-great-great-granddaughter of Thomas Jefferson — a fact that might conceivably account for the garden and the elegant planting around the house.

The present owner made extensive renovations when she bought the house in 1966 and has maintained the grounds exquisitely in this delightful seaside setting.

The lovely English sunken garden room in the shape of a Union Jack borders a broad sweep of lawn that slopes down to Edgartown Harbor. In the foreground, beside a series of roughhewn stone steps leading down to the formal garden, is a small spring garden, with a row of hybrid tea roses on the right, a palette of brilliant color all summer.

A section of the garden, showing the pink and white fibrous begonias at the point of each wedge, backed by spikes of blue veronica, potentilla, and for touches of white, marguerites, and daylilies. Moonbeam coreopsis is interplanted with the potentilla to maintain the color scheme throughout the summer.

Tiger lilies along the back fence.

Right: *A colorful section of the garden, with yellow marguerites and red dahlias in the foreground, and pink lythrum, blue Pacific hybrid delphinium, and dahlias in the background.*

Captain Eric Gabrielson House

———◆———

EDGARTOWN

When Captain Eric Gabrielson was commanding officer of the United States revenue cutter *Gallatin* in the mid–nineteenth century, his vessel often put in at Edgartown. After retiring from sea duty, he decided to settle here and bought this North Water Street house, built in the 1850s. While Gabrielson himself had a distinguished career at sea, it was his Chinese cabin boy, Charles Soong, who would achieve particular recognition. One of Soong's daughters became Madame Chiang Kai-shek, and the other was married to Sun Yat-sen, the Chinese revolutionary.

In 1956 Hope Whipple, of New York City, purchased this architecturally transitional house, with Victorian etched glass doors and Greek Revival trim. She has done extensive redecorating both of the main house and of the charming guesthouse at the rear of the property. She added a lovely side porch that looks out over her sumptuous perennial garden, one of the Island's loveliest, which runs down either side of the rectangular lawn and bursts with color all summer long. August-blooming rose of Sharon bushes and pots of geraniums decorate the front porch.

Pink, green, and lavender predominate in the living room's comfortable sofas, stuffed chairs, curtains, and pillows. The colorful still life over the mantel is by the late Michael O'Shaughnessy, a resident of France and the Vineyard. The Ridgeway china plates and dark-blue Sevres vases highlight the blues in the painting. A pair of Audubon prints hang between the windows; the lamp bases on the end tables are nineteenth-century China trade Peach Blossom balustrade vases. The needlepoint on the stool in the foreground and on the pillows was done by the owner, whose exquisite garden also provided all the flowers for the arrangements: pale pink roses, lady's-mantle, artemisia, coralbells, and the English wildflower astringia.

Right: In the master bedroom, soft blue wallpaper sprinkled with white scallop shells blends with a delightful flowered print used on a chaise longue, curtains, pillows, and a dust ruffle.

The long rug in the front hall, which runs from the entrance to the dining room, was made by the late George Wells of Glen Head, Long Island, as was the rug in the dining room itself.

Right: *China designed by Lynn Chase, called Scenes from the Water's Edge, is ideal for a summer dinner party; a bouquet of dahlias, coreopsis, achillea, rubrum lily, blue platycodon, and white loosestrife from the garden comple-ments the wonderful sherbet colors in the room.*

In the dining room there is another vivid Michael O'Shaughnessy painting and a collection of Ridgeway plates on the sideboard, a Williamsburg reproduction by Kittinger. The flower arrangements include coreopsis, orange geum, daylilies, yellow loosestrife, and red floribunda roses from the garden.

French doors in the living room open onto this cheerful side porch awash in summer colors. The magnificent garden extends the length of the property; the guesthouse is just visible to the rear. Here, a watering can is filled with yellow yarrow, bachelor's buttons, red and pink roses, red bee balm, coreopsis, and viburnum leaves.

Left: Hope Whipple's garden is known for its unusual plants, such as these passionflowers, seen here on a colorful mosaic tile table made by the late Lisa Lineaweaver, a Vineyard artist.

A rose arbor serves as an entryway from the brick sidewalk to this section of the garden. White cosmos, red bee balm (which attracts hummingbirds), hollyhocks, coreopsis, white and blue campanula, pink phlox, and other favorite flowers of Hope Whipple fill the long borders.

Right: Hope Whipple's poodle Katy jumps off the stone bench adjacent to the border filled with phlox, 'Bristol Fairy' baby's breath, platycodon, red bee balm, spiky blue Russian sage, coreopsis, and campanula.

The O'Brien House

EDGARTOWN

North Water Street's historic houses are the most elegant in the village. Built during the whaling era, they are renowned for their handsome doorways, crisp white exteriors, roses tumbling over fences, neatly trimmed boxwood, and flags flying everywhere, a reminder of the Island's maritime heritage.

Mr. and Mrs. Frank O'Brien of Boston use their house year-round. Sometimes, in the quiet of winter, snow "ghosts" the landscaping edging the lawn that slopes down to the waterfront, offering up a stark contrast to the somber, gray-green sea. In summer, the view from the porch provides a fascinating panorama of sailboats and motor boats moving in and out of the harbor, the Chappaquiddick ferry darting back and forth, and the setting sun coloring the cliffs across the outer harbor.

The lush green lawn, bordered by hedges of abelia, leads down to the owner's dock and beach, where the seawall is brightened by the rugged native rugosa rose and blue vitex. Borders of colorful perennials are set against the white fencing that encloses the property.

The charming gazebo is used to store boating and beach equipment for this large, active family, with children and grandchildren who come to visit all summer long. The fan over the door and the porthole window are delightful architectural touches. A pink and blue hydrangea can be seen in the foreground, and the top of Edgartown's town dock, with flags flying, appears in the background.

Opposite above: *The entrance to this handsome Georgian Colonial house, a reproduction built in the 1920s, has a closed pediment over the door, a filled-in fanlight, antique carriage lights, and traditional boxwood lining the walkway.*

Opposite below: *From the owner's dock, a view up the lawn to the house. The weather vane represents a gaff-rigged schooner.*

Emily Post House

—— ◆ ——

EDGARTOWN

In the late 1920s Emily Post, authority on etiquette to millions of Americans, bought this charming early 1800s cottage, located just a few blocks from Edgartown's center.

She added several rooms and an adjacent guest quarters that is connected to her bedroom by a second-story walkway, forming a visually pleasing archway. She also installed a roof walk (often erroneously called a widow's walk — after all, a widow would hardly be looking for the return of her husband's ship!) that affords a breathtaking view of Edgartown Harbor, the town itself, and Chappaquiddick.

Mrs. Post's interest in architecture stemmed from her father, Bruce Price, a well-known architect and the principal designer of Tuxedo Park in New York, where his daughter spent her winters. This little Edgartown house was always her favorite, and she delighted in furnishing it with antiques and decorating it in bright colors to complement the splendid cottage garden.

A wreath of 'New Dawn' roses on the garage/guesthouse is underplanted with hosta.

The colorful cottage garden, filled with several varieties of phlox, Shasta daisies, bee balm, and dahlias, leads to the front door.

The Boathouse

———✦———

EDGARTOWN

Three small boathouses were joined together in the 1920s to make this cottage, which was bought in the 1960s by Stuart and Jean Sutphin, who divide their time among Cincinnati, Florida, and Edgartown. In 1978 the Sutphins had the house moved back fifty feet from the shoreline and raised on cement pilings to protect it from storm damage.

The view from one end of the long porch, decorated with bright-red geraniums, shows boats at their moorings in the inner harbor. The gray shingled building in the background is the Edgartown Reading Room, a private club.

A shell-encrusted mirror hangs over the Victorian mantel, behind Jean Sutphin's arrangement of rubrum lilies, her favorite flower, and part of a shell collection from the Sutphins' winter home in Sanibel, Florida.

Left: A pair of hurricane lamps rest on the sideboard at the dining end of the large living room. Another of the owner's bouquets, on the Ficks-Reed table, includes rubrum lilies, delphiniums, and dahlias.

The colorful living room reflects a very personal style and sensitivity, blending the old with the simply charming. The painting by Sara Wellington, a Phoenix artist, is of the beach and Jean Sutphin's favorite flowers. An antique brass meat scale and a model of the Gloucester schooner Rex, built in Essex, Massachusetts, in 1908, illustrate the owners' flair for mixing delightful artifacts. Jean Sutphin loves to arrange flowers and here has chosen dahlias, morning glories, zinnias, and snapdragons to decorate an antique side table.

A cement sea gull watches over the Sutphins' dock, where the Sutphin children and grandchildren keep their boats. The teak chair originally came from the ocean liner Queen Elizabeth II.

A colorful guest room with an oil painting by the late Bill Abbe, former teacher at Saint Paul's School and Island summer resident, showing Edgartown Harbor before World War II and the town dock without an upper deck.

The porch, done in red, white, and blue with old wicker chairs, is only steps from the beach, and ducks waddle up to be fed every afternoon. On the right is a large ship's lantern. A pair of Chinese garden seats serve as end tables, and flanking the red geraniums on the fireplace, which is used for outdoor parties in summer, are two antique Moroccan lamps.

Edgartown Roses

"Think of the glory of color! The red of the rose . . . ," Celia Thaxter wrote in *An Island Garden*. So it is in Edgartown, which is justly famous for its profusion of soft- and vibrant-colored roses spilling over the white picket fences and framing the town's handsome historic houses. Yellow, peach, white, fiery-red 'Blaze', and soft-pink 'New Dawn' blossoms (the hardy favorite in this coastal village) are all touched with pearls of dew on still, foggy days or in the early morning, when their fragrance fills the sea air.

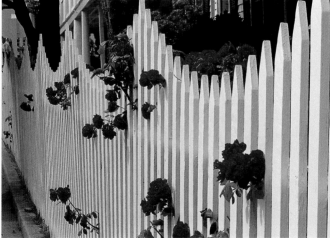

The Ross House

EDGARTOWN

Mr. and Mrs. E. Burke Ross, Jr., of New Jersey and Palm Beach, recently purchased this large Shingle Style house on a high bluff overlooking Edgartown Harbor. Built in the early twentieth century, it affords a spectacular view of the town, Chappaquiddick Island, and, across Nantucket Sound, Cape Cod. All the rooms have been redecorated in glorious summer shades, reflecting the owners' and the decorator's exquisite taste and originality. They completely remodeled the kitchen and made several other structural changes but always managed to preserve the spirit of the place.

A view of the turn-of-the-century Shingle Style houses on the bluff.

The rooms have a light, airy ambience thanks to the ubiquitous water views. This corner of the living room features Edgartown artist Linda Carnegie's unique portrait of the four Ross children.

Left: The house bursts with summer activity for the Rosses' four children and the many guests who fill the guesthouse, the main house, and the boathouse, with its extra bedroom, kitchenette, bath, and fireplace. Here, preparations for a beach picnic wait to be loaded into the family's Boston Whaler.

Right: *The Vose boathouse, in the background, has been a fixture in the harbor since 1899 and is used for parties and storing boating equipment. The porch of the Rosses' boathouse, meanwhile, is filled with summer sports equipment for this active family.*

Two contemporary Vineyard artists created this delightful dining room. Linda Carnegie's mural of Edgartown Harbor in 1900 wraps around the room; John Thayer's dining-room table and the chairs, all grain-painted in a soft blue-green, harmonize beautifully. The ship's model represents a brig of war and dates from about 1920.

The fireplace wall shows the town's waterfront, with some whimsical details. The tiles in the original fireplace surround were also painted by Linda Carnegie, in a shade that matches the owner's lovely green dinner china. The white pickled floors and white wainscoting and trim highlight the artwork and the lovely fabrics used in the room.

Sporting equipment and a settee fill the niche left in the front hall by the new spiral staircase, which winds up to the third floor.

Linda Carnegie's charming artwork decorates cupboards, walls, ceilings, and furniture through- out the house, such as the headboard on this guest-room bed, piled high with lush layers of lace and calico.

William Wise House

———◆———

EDGARTOWN

In small New England towns, old houses are usually referred to by the name either of the original owner or of a prominent individual who owned the house at one time. William Wise of Paris, Texas, built this large Shingle Style house in the 1880s, on a plot located on Edgartown's outer harbor. The present owner, who bought the house in 1960, enlisted landscape designer Edwina vonGal (who also creates displays for Rockefeller Center) to plan the gardens, using both native plants and unusual perennials.

The brick terrace, encircled by 'Forever Pink' hydrangeas, provides a spectacular view of Edgartown's outer harbor, the lighthouse, and Chappaquiddick Island. The Chappaquiddick Beach Club's colorful cabanas are visible at the far right.

The deep-pink flowers along the path in the foreground are 'Roseus' Centranthus.

82

Left: *The cutting garden between the breakfast room and the cobblestoned entrance court is divided into separate blocks of color that provide the house with fresh flowers all summer long. 'Forever Pink' hydrangeas, red alcea hollyhocks, and yellow heliopsis surround the arbor, which is covered with 'White Dawn', red 'Queen Elizabeth', and pink 'Dorothy Perkins' climbing roses.*

Right: *A bird temple overlooks 'Forever Pink' hydrangeas, which have a lavender hue, and yellow 'Summer Sun' heliopsis.*

Below: *'Blue Lace' hydrangea.*

Major's Cove

EDGARTOWN

"We haven't been able to come up with a name for the architectural style," admits the co-owner of this stunning contemporary house overlooking Sengekontacket Pond and the sea beyond. "It has some elements of the Shingle Style, but in a courtyard configuration. The home of Carl Larsson, the Swedish painter, inspired some elements of the interiors, as did the work of several California architects at the turn of the century."

It was the Vineyard's scenic beauty that first inspired Howard Pifer III and Ellen Macke, both Boston executives, to look for property on the Island. After choosing this recently developed area (much of it was originally farmland) on the pond that stretches from Oak Bluffs to Edgartown, they turned to Nan Brinkley, of Brinkley Ford Associates in Boston, to work out the design as well as the interior.

The gray and white shingle style of the exterior contrasts sharply not only with the vivid colors of the interior but also with the play of color and form in the exquisite geometric cottage garden.

Matching vases filled with peach floribunda roses, hosta, and artemisia are displayed on pedestals at either end of the mantel, where they enhance the handsome blue-tile fire surround.

Left: Blue and rust are favorite country colors; Ellen Macke found these richly colored tiles in a magazine and had the ceiling sponge-painted to match. The French doors open onto a large deck that looks out over marshland, a tidal pond, and Sengekontacket Pond. The handsome refectory table, which can seat up to fourteen, was also designed by Brinkley Ford Associates. The antique brass chandelier casts a soft, subtle light on the table, showing off flower arrangements such as this stunning bouquet of delphiniums, artemisia, orange kniphofia, blue agapanthus, white snapdragons, Japanese contorted pussy willow, hosta, and ligularia leaves.

The uniform color scheme flows through from the elegant living room to the kitchen area, with its counter and stools. The sculpture on the coffee table is by Washington, D.C., artist Ella Tulin. Ellen Macke acted as her own decorator, furnishing the house with an eclectic mix of English and Danish pine, traditional Italian, and country Chinese, in a perfect reflection of her very personal style and exquisite taste.

Throughout the house, the ceilings are all beadboard fir, stained to add richness and warmth to the rooms.

Above: *In the colorful cottage garden, each section is edged with dwarf boxwood. The wedge on the right contains purple perennial salvia and pink roses, while the left-hand area has tufts of pink annual celosia, soft blue spikes of Russian sage, Shasta daisies, a scattering of snapdragons, and pink lythrum and coneflower against the garage. The weathered gray arbor is covered in summer with a pink clematis and in the early fall with the white 'Sweet Autumn' clematis.*

Below: *Peastone and flagstone blanket the courtyard entryway.*

Above: From the breezeway, the beautiful courtyard cottage garden. Astilbe, snapdragons, salvia, roses, Russian sage, and daisies are in the traditional English color scheme of pink, blue, and white.

Opposite: A basketful of baby's breath, snapdragons, and astilbe rests on the arbor's garden bench, with soft blue hydrangeas in the background.

"One of my favorite rooms is the courtyard where we have breakfast on summer mornings," says Ellen Macke. Peastone and flagstone are used for this large area at the back of the house, which is adjacent to an exceptionally lovely garden with roses cascading over the arbor and lattice fencing.

Left: The owners collect pottery and commissioned this handsome geometric pattern from the Grazia Pottery Company of Italy, basing the design on a motif they admired in an Italian painting. An arrangement of pink stock, delphinium, orange snapdragons, and lady's-mantle picks up the colors in the placemats and tableware.

Vincent Farmhouse

———•◆•———

EDGARTOWN

Out on the flat, outwash plains along the Island's South Shore at Katama, in Edgartown, there were many small dairy farms in the eighteenth century, each with enough acreage to graze cattle. Extremely self-sufficient, the owners of these farms sold milk, fished in season, raised sheep for wool and mutton, stored their vegetables in root cellars to carry them through the winter, and fashioned their farm tools on anvils.

Built by a member of the Vincent family, one of the Island's earliest settlers, the house dates from between 1690 and 1720. It has undergone some renovation and restoration over the last three hundred years; plumbing and electricity were installed in 1950.

Robert Hughes, an investment banker from Santa Barbara, California, whose grandfather owned several farms in the area, spent his childhood summers on the Island. He and his wife, Susan, bought the house in 1988 and have carefully preserved all its historic charm.

The driveway leading to the farmhouse.

*The focal point of the living room is the fireplace.
The original paneled wall above it surmounts a
simple mantelpiece and pilaster surround that
were added much later, in the late eighteenth or
early nineteenth century. The Windsor rocking
chair is a reproduction.*

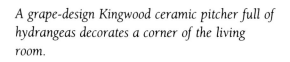

A grape-design Kingwood ceramic pitcher full of hydrangeas decorates a corner of the living room.

This handsome mantelpiece in the master bedroom, with dentil molding and fluted pilasters, was installed in the eighteenth or early nineteenth century. Beach memorabilia collected by the children, a spray of greens and lavender, and sedum 'Autumn Joy' add subtle color.

Right: *Stark simplicity marked both the life-style and the craftsmanship of the early settlers. This gunstock-type hand-carved beam is in one of the bedrooms.*

93

Hereford beef cattle from a nearby farm graze in front of the Hugheses' farmhouse.

A bucket of chrysanthemums rests beside the roughhewn kitchen doorstep.

Left: Zinnias, phlox, and sunflowers in a kitchen window.

An early-autumn picnic on an old sawbuck table
outside the kitchen door.

The Radford House

—◆—

CHAPPAQUIDDICK

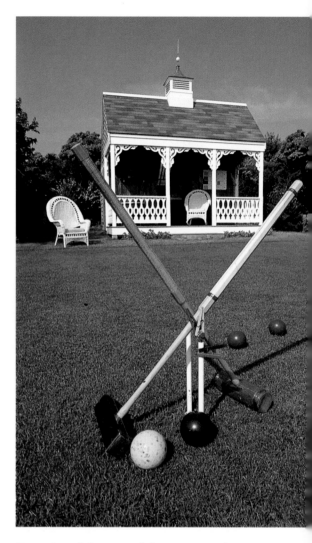

When Earle and Liliane Radford, residents of Kansas City, bought the house in 1969, it was just a tiny one-room shore station for an avid New York sailor who spent time in Edgartown in the 1920s and 1930s. He used it as a respite from days at sea; nearby he built a tiny one-room guesthouse.

Over the years the Radfords enlarged and expanded the main house and guesthouse. Earle Radford, a retired advertising executive who is also an artist, built a studio for himself and recently added a heated pool. The attractive landscaping attests to his keen sense of design.

Evocative of the turn of the century, when croquet was a national pastime, the professional croquet court is the setting for lovely summer garden parties and keen competition.

A view of the main house from the Radfords' dock on Edgartown Harbor.

Located on a high bluff overlooking Edgartown's inner harbor, the living-dining area takes its character from the owners' eclectic mix of antiques, inherited family pieces, and comfortable, contemporary furniture. The antique rocking horse rests on a trunk that Earle Radford's uncle had made for a trip to Alaska in 1900, with a special compartment for his top hat. The dining-room chairs were also inherited, and a bouquet of zinnias and sunflowers decorates the end table, an old ice cream machine. The living room opens onto a large deck, where one can watch sunsets that are a constantly changing display of brilliant colors.

Up-Island

LAMBERT'S COVE

NORTH AND WEST TISBURY

CHILMARK

GAY HEAD

Pilot Hill Farm

——◆——

LAMBERT'S COVE

Marc and Laurie Brown, authors and illustrators of children's books, bought this 1735 farmhouse, which required massive restoration, in 1988. For years it was the home of the internationally renowned oceanographer Columbus Iselin, director of the Woods Hole Oceanographic Institution. Every day, winter and summer, Iselin commuted to Woods Hole from his dock on the North Shore in his forty-foot boat, *Risk,* its design based on that of a Prohibition-era rumrunner.

Marc Brown was his own architect on the yearlong project, which necessitated renovating walls, reshingling, plumbing, wiring, and replacing doors and flooring, "all the while trying to be sensitive to the age and architectural integrity" of the house, for which he and his wife have great respect. Laurie Brown contributed all the design ideas.

Speaking of his love for this charming historic treasure, Marc observes, "It's like a sculpture that you live in. It's a form of creative work, but you have the added benefit that you get to live in the space while you're working on it."

Another creative outlet for Marc Brown is, of course, his enormously successful children's tales about the aardvark Arthur, whose latest adventures have sprung to life in these elegant surroundings.

In order to get the proper sun in this secluded spot deep in the woods, but a stone's throw from the Vineyard Sound, Laurie put the charming raised kitchen garden by the front door.

Left: The old stable, where Marc and Laurie plan to put a studio/gallery space.

The rugged retaining stone walls trailing here and there on the farm are both aesthetically pleasing and functional, separating landscaped from woodland areas. A collection of antique quilts dry on the line.

Left: Both the living room and the dining room open onto a cool shaded terrace furnished with Adirondack chairs, weathered to a driftwood gray, and a delightful stick tea cart. A woodland path leads down to the shore.

A stunning antique French bread cage rests on
an old ice chest in the living room, and an old
basket full of Queen Anne's lace from the garden
has pride of place on a rustic pedestal.

Left: Many of the floors in the house were made
of plywood; the Browns replaced them with
eighteenth-century planks, hand-painted in a
repeating geometric design. They were secured
with new square nails, which Marc found were
still being produced by a factory in Wareham,
Massachusetts. Some of the owners' collection of
ironstone is displayed on the eighteenth-century
mantel, another antique find. The nineteenth-
century pie safe in the corner is in its original
blue paint.

Watching over the butler's pantry is an architectural ornament from an urban building in Erie, Pennsylvania, where Marc Brown grew up. The large gameboard dates from the nineteenth century.

Left: *The antique vegetable bin in the kitchen overflows with comestibles; above it, antique gameboards mingle with spongeware bowls and other kitchen items.*

A nook in the kitchen holds a selection of
miniature toys for the Browns' young daughter.

Left: *The Browns own many fine Windsor
chairs; this one still has its original grape design,
suggestive of the Island. Pie-making is one of
Marc Brown's hobbies.*

An old wicker side table in the dining room was hand-painted. Marc added the arrangement of sunflowers and native wineberries from the garden.

Marc has been collecting Early American antiques since he was twelve years old, and every room in the house reflects his superb taste. The gold-leaf 1840s mirror in the dining room hangs over an original fireplace. The table is a contemporary piece, made by a friend, while the chairs, with their shell motif, date from the 1830s. The diamond-patterned floor was hand-painted and hand-rubbed in subtle shades of soft tan.

An herb-drying rack in the front hall provides a background for a simple arrangement of curly pussy willow and dried leaves. The old farm work table is in its original paint; the rabbit-ear Windsor chair next to it is from the Browns' large collection.

In the first-floor guest room, part of the original house, an exquisite child's wicker high chair stands next to a jelly cupboard crowned with an old copper washtub in its original paint, filled with native grasses.

Left: Even the Browns' bathroom testifies to their love of antiques. The medicine cabinet and sink are from a bygone era, and the antique table and towel rack still retain their old gray-green paint.

In this guest room, part of the original 1735 structure, a bed just fits under the eaves. The cozy room also contains a gameboard, an old set of library steps that serves as a bedside table, a log cabin quilt, and an antique deacon's bench.

Below: *The antique brass bed in the master bedroom came with the house. The collection of hand-colored etchings of shells over the mantel provide a subtle counterpoint to the creamy walls. Laurie's superb sense of color is responsible for the blend of Williamsburg greens and browns and Shaker yellows and reds found throughout the house. The ironstone pitcher on the hearth is part of the Browns' large collection.*

Mohu

—◦•◦—

LAMBERT'S COVE

Elegant and serene, the interior of the North Shore estate of Katharine Graham, chairman of the Washington Post Company, is as beautiful as the surrounding natural terrain of rolling fields, ponds, marshland, and meandering shoreline.

Sited on a high bluff overlooking sea and shore, and the Elizabeth Islands in the distance, the house was, according to the owner, "a tumble-down wreck" when she bought it, in 1972. There was a tennis court, a tennis house, a five-car garage, and a small shell of a house at the tide's edge, but everything needed to be painted, restored, and redecorated. The major structural change was the addition of a large deck that stretches across the back of the house, but a completely new kitchen and bath were also put in, and the bedroom wings were remodeled.

Originally, the house was a very small bungalow bought by Senator William Butler of New Bedford, Massachusetts, in 1911. The thirteenth child of a minister in that old whaling town, Butler entered politics at an early age and eventually became president of the Massachusetts State Senate, chairman of the Republican National Committee, a United States senator, and a prosperous businessman. His success in the textile industry enabled him to enlarge his Vineyard house, where he and his wife entertained many political dignitaries, including the Calvin Coolidges. Butler is reputed to have been largely responsible for Coolidge's election to the presidency.

Today the tradition of Mohu (named for an Algonquin Indian chief) is carried on in this peaceful, sylvan setting. Mrs. Graham is an avid tennis player, a voracious reader, and a renowned hostess. She enjoys entertaining her son and his family, who live nearby, as well as diplomats and other prominent political figures. All find the air of relaxed calm and the sophisticated simplicity of the surroundings charming. And for their hostess, Mohu always provides a welcome escape from the swirl of social activity and the demands on her time in Washington.

The rose-covered porte cochere over the circular drive marks the entryway to Mohu, replacing a heavy front porch. In late spring, the espaliered wisteria edging the roofline is in full bloom.

Left: A dirt road winding under a canopy of conifers and deciduous trees leads past a charming old pergola built in the early 1900s.

Right: A view of Mohu from the beach, with the familiar marsh grasses in the foreground.

Light in tone and spirit, the ambience of the
large, beautifully proportioned blue and white
living room reflects the owner's exquisite taste.
Low stuffed chairs and sofas, some from Mrs.
Graham's family, enhance the relaxed
atmosphere. Tones of sea and sky are
everywhere; the pale-blue ceiling, white curtains
and walls, modern art in shades of blue, and
glass lamps are the epitome of unaffected taste
and comfort.

Opposite below: A painting by Gene Davis
graces the front entrance hall, which opens onto
the library on the right. The hallway to the left
leads to the large living room. Each room has its
own particular aesthetic, but there is a flow of
color from one to the next. The antique folding
screen in the corner provides a background for
Mrs. Graham's silk clivia plant.

Two round tables in the large, airy dining room seat eight each. The antique botanical prints against the soft white walls are well suited to this country setting, and the branches of Kousa dogwood from the property continue the delicate floral theme, making ideal low centerpieces for a dinner party. The colorful napkins pick up the colors in the basket of flowers on the Victorian side table: pink anemones, hybrid delphinium, orange poppies, yellow Anthemis, and white marguerites. The collection of hats in the front hall is useful as well as decorative.

Art and nature come together at Mohu, with
modern art everywhere and views of woodland,
sea, and shore from every window. Next to the
ever-present pile of books on Mrs. Graham's
bedside table, an arrangement of peach
grandiflora roses, yellow yarrow, feverfew, white
snapdragons, lady's-mantle, yellow daisies, and
the pink wildflower saponaria highlights the
colors in the fabrics used throughout the room.

In the hallway leading to the bedroom wings is a
wicker hamper for beach towels, paddleball
equipment for grandchildren, and a collection of
rocks and shells from the beach.

The game room is part of the original house bought by Senator Butler in 1911. A contemporary weather vane and small arrangements of blue bachelor's buttons, feverfew, calendula, and zinnias brighten the whitewashed fieldstone fireplace. Ping-Pong games provide a welcome diversion during nor'easters.

Chip Chop

---◆---

LAMBERT'S COVE

Chip Chop, designed by the architect Eric Gugler for the actress Katharine Cornell in 1937, blends easily into a coastal landscape of dunes and beach grasses. The centerpiece is the large living room, with its wall-sized windows that slide open to the ocean on one side and a large tidal pond on another. Here, theater greats such as the Lunts, Rex Harrison, Laurence Olivier, and Noël Coward did readings of their favorite plays.

While carefully preserving the architectural integrity of the house, the current owners, Leslie and Edmund Glass, added a new master bedroom and studio in what was formerly an attic storage space, opening up dramatic new views, and remodeled the kitchen in the main house. Leslie added a kitchen garden. The house has two charming guest cottages that are connected to the building by a timbered pergola and a garage cottage. With its guesthouses, pool, cabana, and vast public spaces, the property lends itself to entertaining, a passion of all of its owners. The house is decorated with a mixture of furniture and objects from the collections of Leslie's parents, Milton and Elinor Gordon, the Glasses, and Katharine Cornell.

The pool, with its driftwood sculpture at one corner, looks out over the North Shore and Vineyard Sound, which is often white with sail on a brilliant summer's day.

Above: *The relationship of the house (seen here from the beach) to the landscape of sea and shore is one of intimate grandeur. Dusty miller and beach grasses billow in the wind in the foreground.*

Left: *Leslie Glass designed the courtyard cottage garden at the entryway, planted with perennials, annuals, and vegetables. In the near corner are herbs; in the center plot, edged with santolina, are lettuce, peas, basil, tomatoes, and artemisia. Sweet peas, trumpet vine, and roses grow along the weathered gray fence. In the background, behind a planter full of artemisia, is a semicircle of lavender and roses; beyond the fence, a grape arbor opens to the dunes. Edmund Glass has a workshop in the garage, where there is also a separate, one-bedroom apartment.*

The rustic pergola, reminiscent of driftwood
washed ashore and bleaching in the sand,
connects the two charming guesthouses. The huge
antique planters are filled with geraniums.

Left: *Seven kinds of wood were used in the construction of Chip Chop, which took seven years to complete. The beams in the large living room, where singing and rehearsals took place, came from an old Canadian barn. The carving over the fireplace represents Aquarius, Katharine Cornell's zodiac sign. The pine drawers on the left form the back of one segment of a three-sided enclosure for a sofa, which faces the fireplace and has built-in cupboards for sheet music and records. Some of the room's furnishings came from Leslie Glass's family, and others belonged to Cornell. The flower arrangements decorating the tables include pink dahlias, lavender, pink and burgundy scabiosa, red and yellow sunflowers, black-eyed Susans, yellow tansy, white loosestrife, and white astrantia.*

Right: *The rooms at Chip Chop take their character from the unusual furnishings and the warmth of the wood paneling. The hutch in the study, with its collection of blue Dresden china, belonged to Leslie Glass's mother. The little white arrangement contains a Casablanca lily and sweet peas, while strawflowers and native beach plum and grape cascade down a pair of wooden pyramids. The country pine table in the foreground supports antique pewter mugs, a shorebird decoy, some blue and white china, and a pottery pitcher filled with peach daylilies, joe-pye weed, blue hydrangeas, pink strawflowers, and white astrantia.*

On the piano in the living room, an exquisite country farmhouse arrangement by Mariko Kawaguchi combines an eclectic assortment of vegetables, fruits, and flowers from the beach and garden: blue hydrangea, orange rosa rugosa hips, native grapes, ripe beach plums, yellow sunflowers, and radishes. A nineteenth-century velvet quilt serves as a backdrop.

The long, rectangular nuns' table used for dinner parties in the living room was purchased by Katharine Cornell shortly after the house was finished; there is a drawer at each place for storing eating utensils and a napkin. The Meissen china was also Cornell's. The low arrangements of violas, trumpet vine, and nasturtiums also include native plants that are used to make jams and jellies: beach plum, rosa rugosa hips, and wild grapes.

The owners recently converted the attic into a
second-floor master bedroom, sticking to the
spirit of Chip Chop in every way and making
only minimal architectural changes when adding
a small porch. An Appalachian quilt layered
with an antique lace covering warms this
appealing waterfront room.

The seating area at one end of the kitchen takes its character from the unusual eighteenth-century Dutch and French chairs, the antique drop-leaf table, and the china. Katharine Cornell's blue china is a mixture of patterns including Blue Willow and the Meissen Onion pattern, while the contemporary Portmierion is the Glasses' everyday china. The fireplace, which can serve as an indoor grill, has metal doors, studded with brass, to close it off.

Tashmoo Farm

———

Built in 1769 by Captain Samuel Look, Tashmoo Farm remained in the same family for nearly two hundred years. A pre-Revolutionary Island landmark, the farm and its old barns were originally a dairy. For the past several decades it has been a riding stable, and for many years a horse show was held each year on the grounds.

The Ablon House

—•—

LAMBERT'S COVE

In the 1980s, many modern houses were built in the mid- and up-Island areas on the western end of Martha's Vineyard; some are nestled into the natural landscape along the shore, while others are sited on the crests of high hills, with spectacular ocean views.

Richard and Margery Ablon, Long Island residents, bought this rambling waterfront house on the North Shore at Lambert's Cove in 1991. Built in the early 1980s, the house needed extensive redecorating and remodeling, for which the new owners turned to Karen Ward of Vineyard Decorators. Ward did all the interior decorating and interior design work, which included changing cupboards and doors and adding a charming screen porch for dining, as well as providing all the furniture and most of the accessories.

The house blends well with the landscape, respecting the natural contours of the terrain. Nothing distracts from the view of sailboats working their way down Vineyard Sound on a bright summer's day, or from the brilliant evening sunsets over the Elizabeth Islands in the distance.

Outside the living room are a Japanese gong and a seating area; a weathered teak bench at the edge of the lawn invites peaceful meditation. Pots of marguerite, vinca, and pink geraniums decorate the deck.

A feeling of relaxing summer ease emanates
from the huge living room, which is decorated in
tones of pink and blue to blend with the colors of
sea, sky, and those extraordinary sunsets. The
rag rug picks up the hues in the comfortable
stuffed chairs and sofas. A telescope at the
window provides a closer look at passing boats,
Cape Cod in the distance, or the Elizabeth
Islands across Vineyard Sound. The striking
flower arrangement has pink flowering ginger,
curly willow, miniature variegated pineapple,
'Flamingo Pink' haliconia, and monstera leaves.

The low, sprawling house is well sited, with sea views from every room, and seems to recede into the coastal landscape. Native scrub oak and pine fringe the cultivated areas of the lawn. In the foreground is the shell of a horseshoe crab, a prehistoric relic that abounds in the shallow waters around the Island.

Left: Even the white marble sunken bathtub has a glorious view of sea and shore. A carved wooden crab holds the bath towels. Outside, along the deck, which stretches the length of the house, are planters of pink geraniums. The flower arrangement has apricot and yellow foxtail lilies, giant alliums, pink and yellow haliconia, 'King and Queen' porteus, and 'Orange Pincushion' porteus.

139

The Ann Dunham House

NORTH TISBURY

A dirt road meandering through dense woods leads to this low, sprawling Cape house built in the early 1700s. The present owners, former New Yorkers, bought the house in 1980 and over the years have done some remodeling, completely redecorated the interior, and added terraces and gardens.

Inside, the house gives off a sense of intimacy common to many old farmhouses, even as it reflects the unique personality and exquisite taste of its owners.

Located in an open, rolling meadow with a freshwater stream and pond in the rear, the house is one of the oldest on the Island. The old stone terraces and walls and the Indian-quarried doorstep, offset with lilacs, apricot trees, wisteria, camellia bushes, and ancient evergreens, harmonize perfectly with the house itself.

A bird cottage in the courtyard garden in front of a camellia bush, one of several on the property.

Below: *From the courtyard at the rear of the house, an old cemetery gate leads to a freshwater stream that runs the length of the property.*

An unusual collection of birds' nests found on the
property decorates an old woodstove, which is
used when there is a power outage in one of the
Island's not-infrequent nor'easters. The blue
robin's eggs at right contrast with the swan and
duck eggs in the nests in the wooden trencher.

The winter living room, added to the original building eighty years ago, contains a delightful mix of colors, fabrics, and antiques that gives off a sense of hospitable intimacy. There is a relaxed sophistication about all the rooms in the house; their low-beamed ceilings temper the scale and lend a casual quality to the elegant furnishings.

On the trefoil ottoman, a tea tray is set before a roaring fire. Bavarian figures grace the old mantel, and a Chinese needlepoint rug picks up the colors in the comfortable stuffed furniture. A gallery of family photographs and an assortment of Staffordshire figures decorate the bookcase.

Above: *Island artist Margot Datz painted the stairway in trompe l'oeil to reflect the house's woodland setting.*

Left: *In a section of the living-room bookcase, a bouquet of rose of Sharon in a French majolica pitcher is surrounded by part of the owners' lovely collection of exquisite porcelain, much of it inherited. On the top shelf is a Staffordshire castle, and beside the flowers is a Danish porcelain rowboat. Staffordshire dogs and a pair of small German Meissen vases adorn the bottom shelf.*

145

The owners' love of antiques is evident in the eclectic combination of an eighteenth-century Italian dining-room table, Chippendale chairs, Early American drop-leaf side table, Italian ivory eagle-head hurricane lamps, and Oriental rug. Shasta daisies from the garden decorate the tables.

The table setting juxtaposes the old and the new: contemporary blueberry-design plates, cut crystal finger bowls for fruit, and lovely Georgian silver candlesticks and salt and peppers.

The kitchen is large but cozy, with areas for sitting and for eating. The table at the dining end picks up the owners' favorite shades of blue in the plates, glasses, and tablecloth. In the foreground is a captain's chair; near the stove, a collection of antique baskets hang from a beam. The colorful bouquet on the bookcase, with flowers from the garden, was arranged by the owner.

The pantry sink looks out over the courtyard and the entrance to the indoor swimming pool, a recent addition. A collection of old blue bottles lines the windowsill, and an old tennis racket decorates the wall.

What is now an office was originally a chicken coop and then a breezeway leading to the master bedroom and baths. Dutch doors open to the front terrace and the back courtyard. A handsome highboy, one of several exquisite pieces in the house, is topped with old baskets.

The collection of quilts on the antique sleigh bed and the hooked rug near the door give the room a relaxed, country feeling.

150

When the owners remodeled the master-bedroom bath, they installed blue Italian tiles and gold-plated fixtures for the bathtub. The soap dish and sponge holder are both antique brass.

Many of the furnishings in the house were inherited; in fact, one of the owners was born in this antique four-poster bed, which came from Barbados. The chest at the foot of the bed is Spanish. The blue-tinted pickled pine floors blend beautifully with the blue and white fabric.

The Schneider Garden

———◆———

WEST TISBURY

Tucked away in a secluded spot in the center of West Tisbury is one of the Island's most beautiful gardens. A broad expanse of lush green lawn slopes down to the Tiasquam River, where ducks and swans raise their young.

Herman and Nina Schneider, both writers, have devoted years to developing and designing this extraordinary property, using great imagination and flair.

The Schneiders' gardens are a wonderland of color, including marigolds in front of the spiky mauve malva, lavender and red dahlias, and the bright hues of deciduous trees in the background, a harbinger of the colder days that lie ahead. In the immediate foreground, antique wrought-iron chairs surround a pedestaled sundial.

The lovely foxglove and yellow iris, on the far left, are reflected in the still waters of the Tiasquam River. Marsh grasses fill the foreground.

Clematis 'Nelly Moser' entwined around a tree, with a view of the lawn sweeping down to the river.

Right: The Schneiders' gardens are carefully planned to coordinate color and time of bloom. In the early fall, pink hollyhocks and red and lavender dahlias brighten the arbored path between the terraced gardens and a fruit orchard, while the red and mauve of deciduous trees edge the property. A dairy farm is visible in the far background, across the Tiasquam River.

PIES
BY
KAREN
PEACH, APPLE,
STRAWBERRY RHUBARB

HILLSIDE FARM
OUR FARM STAND IS
OPEN DAILY
STATE RD.
N. TISBURY
693-5851

Farmers' Market

———◆———

A new and extremely popular summer fixture is the farmers' market held every Saturday morning from June to September at the fairgrounds in West Tisbury. Farmers from all over the Island display their produce, while others sell baked goods, jellies, jams, crafts, plants, and fresh flowers, all Island-made or -grown.

Sweet Meadow

———•———

WEST TISBURY

West Tisbury, in mid-Island, has always been known as a farming community. This unusual hip-roofed Georgian Colonial house, located in a lovely pastoral setting with a commanding view of gently sloping land reaching down to Mill Brook in the back, is an exceptionally handsome example of the area's historic buildings.

The original house, built in the early 1700s, was half the size of the present building; in 1848 it was greatly enlarged but nonetheless managed to retain its architectural integrity and its spirit. The renovation included the installation of sidelights in the front-door surround and the addition of a kitchen ell, formerly part of the old Dukes County Academy. The school, located in the center of town, was attended by many grown whalemen who had missed school when they were young.

Lawrence and Carol Brandon, former New Yorkers who spend part of the year in France, inherited the house in 1951. Filled with antiques, it is decorated in a manner that shows respect and admiration for its 250-year history.

There are several lovely perennial gardens on the property. June-blooming Shasta daisies, Oriental lilies, 'Jackmanii' clematis, and stock fill a section of a border against the garage, where a collection of old baskets is visible through a window.

The symmetry of the house reflects its original Georgian design.

Right: *Carol Brandon is an avid gardener and worked for several years to develop this striking heather hillside, which includes white 'Martha Herman', pink 'J. H. Hamilton', yellow 'Gold Haze', and lavender 'Blaze Away', as well as 'Springwood' white heath, which blooms from January to April. The bunkhouse in the background, formerly a chicken coop, is used by visiting grandchildren during the summer.*

With its square rooms and wonderful blend of antiques, fabrics, and patterns, the house emanates a sense of warmth and intimacy common to many Early American houses. The fireplace is the focal point of the living room, with its Ingram steeple clock, Staffordshire figures, and Early American brasses. Carol Brandon's vase of lilies, hydrangea, and snapdragons rests on the Franklin stove; to the left, in the built-in cupboard, is a collection of Rose Medallion plates. The landscape over the sofa dates from the 1930s. In the background is the music room, with an Early American rush-seat chair below the Seth Thomas banjo clock.

Right: In the music room, an oil painting of the Gay Head cliffs hangs above a collection of old chocolate molds. The bouquet of red and yellow Oriental lilies is from the owner's garden.

161

The elegance of wood, darkened by age, sets the tone for this charming kitchen area with pine paneling that was once part of the old Dukes County Academy. The fruit basket rests on a sawbuck table made by the late Roger Allen, a well-known Chilmark artisan who built the steeple for the Chilmark Methodist Church. Kerosene lamps (a necessity when a nor'easter causes a power outage), a Shaker box, and a pottery jar filled with Shasta daisies, Oriental lilies, butterfly weed, petunias, and snapdragons decorate the Early American drop-leaf table in the background.

162

Antiques fill the guest rooms; here, a spool bed, a Meissen figurine of a clown on an Early American pine bureau, and an antique rocking chair set the scene. The delicate pattern of the wallpaper is picked up by the matching dust ruffle; at the foot of the bed, a contemporary chest made by Edward Hewitt, a well-known Vineyard craftsman, completes the period-piece setting.

Right: Simple blue-painted wooden floors provide a colorful background for the rag-rug stair runner and the old hooked rugs used throughout the house.

Barnard's Inn Farm

NORTH TISBURY

The late Harold Bruce, curator of plants at Winterthur, wrote in a tribute in the July 1982 issue of *Horticulture* magazine, "Polly Hill has done what very few Americans have. She has had the patience to grow all sorts of things from seed, and has lived long enough to select the best of them. . . . She has made quite a considerable contribution to horticulture."

Polly Hill is known throughout the country for the work she has done with azaleas, rhododendrons, camellias, hollies, and other plants on the twenty acres of open farmland she has landscaped and developed in North Tisbury. A number of her hybrids are now available in the trade.

Polly took over the management and nurturing of the farm, her family's summer house, from her parents in the late 1950s. She and her husband, Julian, who is now retired, spend winters in Hockessin, Delaware.

Barnard's Inn Farm, a stagecoach stop in the nineteenth century, is an extraordinary Island treasure that reflects the expertise and sparkling personality of its owners. It is open to the public. Don't be surprised if you see Polly scooting around the property in her electric cart, shovels and rakes piled in the back!

The June-blooming Cornus Kousa cultivar 'Big Apple', one of eight dogwoods that Polly Hill has introduced to the trade.

Polly Hill's twenty-acre arboretum at Barnard's Inn Farm includes several barns as well as magnificent open fields, woodlands, and stone walls, which outline various areas of unusual plantings on the property.

"I think the most beautiful things here are the stone walls. I'm not sure I would have started the arboretum without them," Polly declares.

One of the most unusual areas is the "playpen," an oblong wire-enclosed arboretum where extraordinary azaleas, rhododendrons, and conifers grow in a peaceful, sylvan setting. In the center are the Robin Hill azaleas, the pink 'Lady Louise', and, on the left, another Robin Hill, the white and pink 'Sara Holdin'. In the foreground is one of Polly's famous North Tisbury azaleas, the late-blooming 'Late Love', which she developed, grew, and introduced to the trade.

The late-blooming 'Gabrielle Hill', another of the North Tisbury azaleas developed and introduced to the trade by Polly Hill.

Right: The delicate blossoms of the Gleam Dale rhododendron 'Ben Morrison' blend with light, airy 'Lady' ferns.

The stunning 'Lazursterne' clematis — developed, grown, and introduced to the trade by Polly Hill — is just one of the many plants, shrubs, and trees distributed throughout the country by her arboretum.

Moon Tide

NORTH TISBURY

For Bertrand Taylor and his late wife, Lisa, the founding director of the Cooper-Hewitt Museum, the Smithsonian's National Museum of Design, this seven-acre promontory overlooking the Island's North Shore was reminiscent of the coast of Japan. It was in Japan, in the 1950s, that Lisa Taylor first met Teruo Hara, an acclaimed potter who later became an architect. She was working on the staff of Dwight Eisenhower's People to People program at the time; the experience, and the friendship, "changed her life," her husband remembers, "because Japan will do that." In 1978, when the Taylors made plans to build, they envisioned their ideal Japanese house and asked Hara to design what they called "our Katsura Palace." The essence that they sought to recapture was the palace's rustic yet refined tranquillity. "Moon Tide is the most rare of accomplishments — the lifetime realization of one man's dream," Mr. Taylor explains about Hara's work. The architect also crafted most of the furnishings and accessories used in the house. A resident of Florida, the owner spends summers in his North Tisbury home, his favorite place, and part of the year in Paris, where he has an apartment.

It took nineteen Japanese and Korean craftsmen four years to complete the buildings and grounds. The house was assembled using traditional Japanese techniques of wood joinery; twenty-three types of wood, with varied hues and grain, enrich the rooms, and every detail was painstakingly completed by hand. But while Hara employed traditional construction methods, he adapted them to his own unique design. Hidden behind Hara's warm wooden surfaces are today's high-tech amenities: electric lights, fire alarms, medicine cabinets, and a television.

Teruo Hara let the natural terrain be his guide in landscaping the steep, rocky promontory. The tea house is nestled among native cedar and pine. The Elizabeth Islands are visible in the background, across Vineyard Sound.

The turkey grit used on the walkway sand garden had to be imported from North Carolina; Vineyard sand contains too much clay for proper raking.

Left: *The walkway stops at the front door, which is on the lower level. The door opens onto an exercise pool that is wrapped in lush green plants and filled with filtered seawater from Vineyard Sound.*

Hara's furniture and pottery are everywhere in the large living room. The room is wrapped in shoji screens, which can slide open to create a larger space; the changing light and shadows that filter through them highlight the rich tones of the wood. A bouquet of miniature eucalyptus, bear grass, and purple butterfly bush is displayed in a pottery vase on the low coffee table, while a larger vase in the foreground holds Japanese pussy willow, burgundy leccodendron, yellow tansy, and orange montbretia.

The room adjacent to the pool area displays a selection of kimonos, or yukatas. Pottery bowls on the tatami mats used throughout the house were made by Hara; the sculpture on the lower right is by the Japanese architect Aiko Isozaki.

Left: *The ceiling in a guest room is covered with native Vineyard phragmites secured with bamboo and strips of redwood, the warm colors blending with the cool, soft gray of the walls, made of clay and fiber.*

Below left: *The andon, or lamp, made of rice paper, redwood, and sugar pine, casts a soft glow over two of Hara's pottery plates and an arrangement of purple butterfly bush, burgundy leccodendron, and blue eryngium.*

Below: *A collection of the late Lisa Taylor's Japanese wooden combs is arranged on a bathroom vanity, with one of Hara's bowls, filled with eucalyptus, dried hydrangea, and orange montbretia in the corner.*

Above: *In the master bedroom, shoji screens open onto a little balcony that looks out over Vineyard Sound. The late-eighteenth-century scroll in the tokonoma, a traditional alcove, is by Mori Sosen, whose life's work it was to paint monkeys. The alcove is decorated with a bowl of burgundy leccodendron, Japanese pussy willow, and white heath. The exquisite interplay of woods is seen in the cypress and redwood ceiling and the rough cedar post.*

Above right: *Hanging from a rafter in the farmhouse kitchen is a cluster of baskets from all over the world, collected by the late Lisa Taylor. Native wood is found in many places in the house, such as this post from a beetlebung, or tupelo, tree.*

Right: *The freestanding stairway leading from the lower level to the living room above celebrates space and provides a geometric counterpoint to a collection of Hara's pottery.*

Down the hill from the main house, near a man-made waterfall and pond, is the tea house, set in a grove of native pine, cedar, and oak trees.

Right: *A screen made of bamboo and clay is used to enclose one end of the little porch.*

Far right: *A latticework system of bamboo mullions fills a window at one end of the tea house's small porch.*

Below: *Inside the tea house, a scroll by the mid-seventeenth-century artist Kano Tenye and a bouquet of viburnum decorate the* tokonoma. *The round pot at left heats water for tea on an open fire.*

Agricultural Fair

For well over a century an agricultural fair and livestock show has been held at the fairgrounds in West Tisbury in August. It was originally held in the fall, after the farmers' crops were in and root cellars had been filled for the long winter ahead. One of the Island's most popular summer attractions, it now includes not only exhibitions of crops and livestock and a pet show, but also a Ferris wheel and other rides, games of chance, a merry-go-round, numerous food booths, a fiddlers' contest, and the crowd-pleasing, century-old favorite, the horse pull.

Brookside Farm

——◆——

CHILMARK

"This was the only house I wanted to live in on Martha's Vineyard," Wendy Gimbel recalls. When she and her husband, Douglas Liebhafsky, were shown this Chilmark farm in 1987, they bought it instantly.

Originally built in the late eighteenth century, the structure was added to over the years and in 1835 became the home of Captain Allen Tilton, former master of the whaleship *Omega* and also of the *Loan*, one of Edgartown's best-known vessels. Like many Island mariners who spent years at sea, Tilton chose to live inland when he came ashore.

The house needed extensive restoration when Gimbel and Liebhafsky bought it, but it was full of country farmhouse charm, with original fireplaces, 12/12 windows, and wide pine flooring. Appreciating the farm's past, the owners chose to preserve the historical accuracy of the interior; their superb taste has resulted in a winning and eclectic combination of the personal and the vernacular.

The magnificent stone walls all had to be repaired when the owners bought the place, and the barns had to be restored. The Red Devon cattle are used in place of oxen, doing heavy moving as necessary on the property.

The appeal of the charming living room is strengthened by the American primitive paintings over the fireplace and the antique rocking horse, both by A. Davies, as well as by the small George Inness landscape in the corner. The colors of the seat and back of the Shaker rocker are picked up in the garden bouquet on the eighteenth-century English oak stretcher table. The unusual folk-art chess set consists of hand-carved chickens, roosters, and other barnyard figures.

Below: Wendy Gimbel and her son Mark are the horseback riders at Brookside Farm. The antique basket rests on an old milking stool that the owners found in the barn when they bought the place.

The spiral stairs — the only modern feature in the house — were installed to allow easier access to the upstairs bedrooms. The dark woods in the sideboard are lightened by a collection of ironstone plates, a bouquet of peonies, a copper kettle, and an old cork-bodied decoy in a basket. The floor is wood, painted in a checkerboard pattern.

An early spool bed and an antique quilt are the focal points in the bedroom of one of Wendy Gimbel's sons. The clipper-ship paintings are by the late Captain John Ivory, who lived on a boat in Vineyard Haven Harbor.

Wendy Gimbel acted as her own decorator, and her taste for Early American antiques is evident everywhere. In the workroom adjacent to the kitchen, buckets of peonies (one of Wendy's favorites), delphinium, lilies, and bachelor's buttons are waiting to be arranged; the clippers are kept in the antique pine spoon rack on the wall.

Local artist Mary Mayhew stenciled the grape design on the kitchen wall.

Missouri Fox Trotters and Red Devon cattle
roam the fields, adding to the farm's bucolic
charm. The little building in the foreground at
left, with its window box of impatiens and
peonies below, is the old milk house, now used as
the farm's office.

Beautiful perennial gardens are everywhere on the farm; this phlox border is at the back of the house. Ducks, horses, and cattle wander freely over the rolling hillside, which drops down to Davis Pond. This is Wendy Gimbel's favorite view of the property.

Almon Stanton Tilton Homestead

— ◆ —

CHILMARK

This early 1800s farmhouse nestles so naturally into the hillside, embraced by magnificent stone walls, that one is tempted to believe it has always been there. But in fact it was moved to this site from Meeting House Road in Chilmark, where it was originally a general store with an upstairs apartment for the local pastor.

Like so many country-style houses, this one, with its beamed ceilings, plaster walls, ancient fireplaces, and accumulation of cherished possessions, is all about comfort and conviviality. Howard Hillman of Greenwich, Connecticut, inherited the property from his mother in the late 1960s, so for him and his wife, Sandra, it is also steeped in family history. Sandra Hillman has her own deep Vineyard roots: she is related to the Island's Cleveland family, several members of which spent years whaling in the Pacific.

A collection of Island treasures — including old handwoven eel traps, an antique wicker chair, and a child's sled — share the barn with the Hillmans' horses, brought up from Greenwich each summer.

*Mid-Island summers differ markedly from those
spent down-Island or along the waterfront. The
kitchen and informal dining room are the heart
of this home. The open cupboards are stacked
with a potpourri of old china, washbasins, and
pitchers.*

A bouquet of flowers from the garden decorates
an old upright piano with an unusual hand-
painted Oriental design, made by the Campbell
Company of New York.

A shell collection lines the stairway.

The beamed ceiling, the handcrafted mantel (made from a fallen cherry tree from Polly Hill's arboretum), and the soft pink of the fireplace's Island-made bricks contribute to the warmth and character of the living room. Like all country farmhouses, this one contains an accumulation of possessions assembled over the years to accommodate the owners' life-style. The flowers in the cobalt-blue vase on the mantel are from the Hillmans' colorful perennial garden.

The casual combining of disparate patterns, objects, and furnishings is typical of a country-style bedroom. A stand, used here as a bedside table, holds books, towels, clothes, and prize ribbons from the Island's annual agricultural fair.

White phlox and nicotiana, two of Sandra Hillman's favorite flowers, brighten a garden bouquet on an old pine bureau in a guest room.

Wade's Cove Farm

———◆———

CHILMARK

When Stuart and Karen Watson, Connecticut residents, bought this Victorian house in 1985, it had been moved back from the road and turned around by the previous owner, who had also begun remodeling it. It was built at the turn of the century by Benjamin Frank Mayhew, a descendant of the Island's founding family. The interior needed extensive work, and the Watsons' interesting renovations have a solid feel, yet the house is light in tone and spirit, with walls and floors washed in soft colors that are well suited to a family with four young children.

The whole back of the house was remodeled with outdoor summer living in mind. With its screened porch, charming wisteria-draped pergola, and flagstone terrace, the back now provides glorious views of a fruit orchard of peach, pear, nectarine, and cherry trees, a huge wildflower garden, and Wade's Cove in the far distance.

In mid-June, toadflax blankets the field, which reaches down to the cove.

Its symmetrical, geometric pattern gives the English garden off the dining room a formal, eighteenth-century aspect. Planters of dwarf Alberta spruce flank the steps to this colorful display of annuals and perennials. Silver mound and pearly everlasting encircle the fountain, made from one piece of alabaster. The vivid loosestrife in the near left corner blends with the soft gray artemisia, the white phlox and snapdragons, the blue salvias, the deep-pink 'Stargazer' lilies, the yellow pansies, and the soft-pink 'Cranesbill' geraniums. The building in the background is the garage.

Out beyond the landscaped area is a charming guesthouse in a spectacular field of Queen Anne's lace, which blooms in midsummer.

An ancient wheelbarrow full of Queen Anne's lace is backed by one of the many handsome stone walls on the property.

Left: *The Italian oak sideboard is decorated and lightened with a collection of French majolica plates and both old and new blue glass.*

Opposite: *The walls and floors in the house are all painted in soft, summery colors, such as the mars violet on the third floor. An old wicker sewing table serves as a nightstand beside the antique painted French bed in Anne Watson's room. The whole family enjoys horseback riding, and Anne's ribbons from Island horse shows line the window.*

Above: *The living room is an attractive blend of antiques, comfortable stuffed furniture, and reminders that children are very much a part of summers at the farm. It was decorated around the colors in the Carolyn Blish painting on the right, above an antique Chinese porcelain chicken. The cedar coffee table is actually an Empire drum table that was cut down; on the far right is a triangular, heavily carved, drop-leaf oak Victorian side table. Antique black iron sconces flank the handsome fireplace surround, which required seven different colors of paint applied with rags, sponges, and a whisk broom. The old botanical prints reflect the colors in the room. In the dining room, in the background, an old electrified candelabra lights an unusual Victorian gateleg table surrounded by oak slat-backed antique chairs.*

Robert A. M. Stern House

———— •• ————

CHILMARK

"This shingled home continues the tradition of the seaside house architecture that emerged in the 1870s along the New England coast," explained architect Robert A. M. Stern when the house was completed, in 1984. Sited on an up-Island hilltop, with a spectacular 180-degree view embracing the South Shore, the Elizabeth Islands, and, in the far distance, Newport, Rhode Island, it is a superb interpretation of the American Shingle Style vernacular revival that became so popular in the 1980s.

The owners first visited the Island in the 1950s, when they made an unplanned stop on a sailing trip. When they decided to build a house, they turned to Stern, whose work they admired. According to Vincent Scully, the noted architectural historian, by the late 1970s Stern "was learning how to build — and decorate — as the original architects of the original Shingle Style had done. . . . This house on Martha's Vineyard is an eloquent and powerful essay in that language."

The wide deck across the back of the house, open to vast panoramic vistas, includes a covered porch with rush-seated rocking chairs and a screened-in porch with a dining area, where most meals are served. The large pool is just below.

The deep inglenook in the center of the living
room makes a fine place for some of the owners'
collection of maritime art; the 1866 painting
of a square-rigged ship over the mantel is by
A. Krapp. Reminders of the sea are everywhere:
the eighteenth-century country French coffee
table holds navigation lights and scrimshaw, and
on the far left, in the hallway leading to the
dining room, is an old engine-room telegraph.

One of the owners' favorite spots is the deck, where they can watch "the changing hues of sunsets over the Elizabeth Islands, the Gay Head light on a dark night, and Newport, Rhode Island, on a brilliantly clear summer's day."

The large round window is one of Stern's signature motifs.

All the walls in the house are finished in beaded vertical board with white trim, providing a simple but elegant background for the owners' art and furnishings. A painting of the oceangoing tug Wallace B. Flint, by Antonio Jacobsen, hangs over the blue-tiled fire surround in the dining room. The rich tones of the antique French stretcher table and the rush-seated ladderback chairs warm the room, and the collection of Quimper ware and other pieces in the open cupboard add sparkle.

Left: The huge ship's figurehead at one end of the living room was formerly in the collection of Barbara Johnson of Princeton, New Jersey. It is from a large sailing vessel, probably a square-rigged ship.

Hilly Mayhew House

——◆——

CHILMARK

Vaclav Vytlacil was one of a group of New York artists and writers who came to Chilmark before World War I, finding affordable lodging in barns and shacks. He was well known in his early years as an interpreter of Cézanne's Modernism, both as a teacher at the Art Students League and in his own work. Later he played an active role in the development of abstractionism, right up through the post–World War II flowering of American art.

Enchanted with the Vineyard's natural beauty and superb light, he continued to summer on the Island throughout his life, teaching regularly at the Old Sculpin Art Gallery in Edgartown. His dynamic personality, humor, and warmth were such that Ruth Galley, a gallery member, recalled, "Every time Vyt came in, everyone would stop working and cluster around him."

In 1928 Vytlacil inherited this little farmhouse overlooking the South Shore, which had at one time belonged to Hilly Mayhew, a well-known Chilmark fisherman. He painted hundreds of Island seascapes and harbor scenes over the next fifty-six years, until his death, in 1984.

The cobalt-blue walls and floors in the living room complement Vytlacil's seascapes and the tones of sea and sky that are visible from every window. The painting on the right is an oil-crayon sketch of Menemsha fishing boats, circa 1970. Both the upholstered chair and the Victorian stool are family pieces; the ceramic ship bas-relief on the fireplace surround was there when Vyt inherited the place.

Above: Rudbeckia, yellow yarrow, tiger lilies, and pink dianthus decorate an antique country maple bureau in the front bedroom that was "probably acquired at some junkshop years ago," according to the artist's daughter. An old ironstone pitcher holds a collection of feathers.

Vytlacil's early Island paintings include a 1918 oil of Menemsha, on the upper right, that shows a Cézannesque influence, and a seascape, on the upper left, that is "clearly related to Winslow Homer," according to the artist's daughter, who now owns the house. Both the early oil of Menemsha on the lower left and the view of the beach and cliffs at Roger Baldwin's place, Windy Gates, on South Beach, again point to the influence of Cézanne on Vytlacil's work.

All the rooms in the house are painted in vivid primary colors to complement the artwork. The living room, as seen from the front bedroom, is furnished with a bench made from a child's Shaker cradle. The abstract painting dates from the 1960s and depicts Menemsha.

The house looks out over Squibnocket Pond and the ocean beyond.

Primary colors pervade the country kitchen as well; the tin bucket of flowers in the old-fashioned sink carries out the vivid color scheme.

Blues and greens also predominate in the bathroom, with the vivid blue picked up in an old washbasin and pitcher filled with lilies, coreopsis, and delphiniums, in Vytlacil's 1970s abstract painting of waves, and in a collection of bottles that Ann Vytlacil found on the property.

213

Menemsha

———— ◆ ————

In the nineteenth century the area just west of Menemsha, called Lobsterville, was the only port on the western end of the Vineyard. It was here, during the fishing season, that smacks would put in daily from New York to buy the fish and lobsters, which cost five cents each. Menemsha, called Creekville at that time, was then just a narrow inlet leading into Menemsha Pond. In 1905 the creek was dredged and riprapped to form the harbor, and the name of the village was changed to Menemsha, which reportedly comes from an Indian word meaning "still water." In its new incarnation, Menemsha quickly became an active fishing port, which it remains today. The fishing boats and fish markets lining the east side of the basin, and the boathouses along the west side — weathered to a silvery gray in the salt air and cluttered with buoys, anchors, rope, and lobster traps — give the little port its character and visual charm, along with the fishermen's ancestral homes up on the bluff behind the harbor.

With the increasing influx of pleasure craft in recent years, a marina was built along the west side of the harbor. Small shops and food stands have opened not far from the old general store, which houses the post office and has been there for a century. The changes were inevitable, but in the end it is the fishing fleet and the boathouses — still used daily for the business of fishing — that make Menemsha so appealing.

215

Sunny Sands

———◆———

GAY HEAD

Lobsterville, on Gay Head's North Shore between Menemsha and the Gay Head lighthouse, was the Island's most important fishing village in the nineteenth century, before Menemsha Creek was dredged to make the present harbor. Numerous boathouses dotted the shore, built by lobstermen and fishermen for use during the warm weather.

Argie Humphrey, who owns Humphrey's Bakery in North Tisbury, an Island landmark, bought Sunny Sands in the 1940s. It is now owned by his daughter and son-in-law, Bernice and Pierce Kirby. The house was built as a two-room fishing camp in the 1920s and survived the 1938 hurricane, in which Menemsha Harbor was completely destroyed; only Sunny Sands' outhouse was swept away.

Furnishings acquired here and there set the tone for the informal living room. The wicker chair has been used by four generations of the Humphrey family to rock babies. A plate of native wild oysters and a bowl of fruit are arranged on a table built by Daniel Manter, a well-known member of an old Vineyard family. Lobster buoys picked up on the shore decorate the mantel above the fireplace, which was made from beach stones.

Right: A collection of lusterware fills a shelf in a bookcase.

A little porch looks out over Vineyard Sound and masses of rugosa rose, which was originally an import from Japan but now grows over dunes all around the Island. The rose hips are used in jam.

Right: Marigolds, beach grasses, and rugosa rose hips decorate a Victorian bureau in the bedroom.

A beach picnic down on the shore.

An inlet on Menemsha Pond, where sailboat
races are held in the summer.

A painted table is covered with a fine collection
of fish decoys and a whale's vertebra that was
found washed ashore and bleaching in the sand
like driftwood.

Credits

Down-Island

VINEYARD HAVEN

Captain Gilbert Smith House:
Flower arrangements, Susan Branch

The Old Seamen's Bethel:
Architect, Jeffrey White
Flower arrangements, Mariko Kawaguchi,
Donaroma Nursery

EAST CHOP

Colossal Fossil:
Interior design, Sage Chase
Architectural restoration, Gary Conover

OAK BLUFFS

Kelly House:
Interior design, John and Sharon Kelly
Flower arrangements, Mariko Kawaguchi,
Donaroma Nursery

EDGARTOWN

Thomas Cooke House:
Flower arrangements, Mariko Kawaguchi,
Donaroma Nursery

Miniscule:
Landscape gardener, Duncan McBride

Captain Eric Gabrielson House:
Landscape gardener, James Klingensmith
Interior decorator, Pam Timmins,
Timmins and Munn
Flower arrangements, Mariko Kawaguchi

Emily Post House:
Landscape gardener, Tony Bettencourt

The Boathouse:
Landscape gardener, Donaroma Nursery
Flower arrangements, Jean Sutphin

Ross House:
Interior decorator, Nancy Haskell
Interior design, Linda Carnegie
Flower arrangements, Mariko Kawaguchi,
Donaroma Nursery
Landscape gardener, Francis Creamer

William Wise House:
Landscape architect, Edwina vonGal and
Company

Major's Cove:
Architect, Nan Brinkley, Brinkley Ford Associates
Interior design, Nan Brinkley, Brinkley Ford
Associates
Landscape architecture, Peter Cummin,
Cummin Associates, Inc.
Flower arrangements, Mariko Kawaguchi,
Donaroma Nursery

CHAPPAQUIDDICK

Radford House:
Landscape design, Earle Radford
Landscape gardener, Donaroma Nursery

Up-Island

LAMBERT'S COVE

Pilot Hill Farm:
Architectural restoration, Marc Brown
Interior design, Laurie Brown
Landscape design, Marc and Laurie Brown
Flower arrangements, Marc Brown

Mohu:
Interior decorator, Robert Perkins
Architect, Don Page
Flower arrangements, Mariko Kawaguchi,
Donaroma Nursery

Chip Chop:
Architect, Eric Gugler
Flower arrangements, Mariko Kawaguchi,
Donaroma Nursery

Ablon House:
Interior decorator, Karen Ward
Interior design, Karen Ward
Flower arrangements, Mariko Kawaguchi,
Donaroma Nursery
Landscape gardener, Robert Clark

NORTH AND WEST TISBURY

Ann Dunham House:
Flower arrangements, the owner
Interior decorator, Trio Interiors
Landscape gardener, Carlos Montoya

Moon Tide:
Architect, Teruo Hara
Interior design, Teruo Hara
Landscape architect, Teruo Hara
Flower arrangements, Mariko Kawaguchi,
Donaroma Nursery

CHILMARK

Brookside Farm:
Interior decorator, Wendy Gimbel
Landscape gardener, Hilary Blocksom

Almon Stanton Tilton Homestead:
Flower arrangements, Lisl Dennis

Wade's Cove Farm:
Interior decorator, Lynda Levy
Interior design, Blaine Forintos
Landscape gardener, Blaine Forintos
Flower arrangements, Lisl Dennis

Robert A. M. Stern House:
Architect, Robert A. M. Stern
Interior decorator, Alan Gerber

Hilly Mayhew House:
Flower arrangements, Lisl Dennis